Cognitive Behavioral Therapy: How It Really Works

All the techniques revealed and explained in depth.

CBT strategies that kill anxiety, depression, phobias and other psychological disorders

By Tom Brain

TABLE OF CONTENTS

INTRODUCTION

Congratulation on downloading your copy of Cognitive Behavioral Therapy. This book will give you finer details about the topic in question without compromising on any crucial information.

A read through the book will make you understand the various techniques that are used for CBT. The aim is to make the readers find all the crucial details of CBT in one read. By the end of reading this book, you should be well-equipped with the necessary tools that govern Cognitive Behavioral Therapy.

The information described in this book is real and accurate. It enlightens the readers based on truthful research and information. The words used in this book are simple; hence, the readers will have a clear understanding of CBT as well as any crucial information that surrounds this topic.

Again, there are plenty of books about CBT, but you have picked this one. Thanks again for making such a decision. This eBook contains relevant information that you'll find very useful. Every effort was made in ensuring that the document features accurate information that won't mislead the readers. Thank you once more for taking your precious time to download this document!

CHAPTER 1: COGNITIVE BEHAVIORAL THERAPY

Cognitive Behavioral Therapy (CBT) creates a direct link between behaviors, thoughts, and emotions. People often find it hard when they are put in a box to change their practices and way of thinking. A rapid change in their lifestyle or way though can lead them into depression, especially when they feel left out. CBT advocates for a gradual process towards restoring the mental health of various patients. This psychotherapeutic process works with the aim of restoring normality unto the lives of different patients. It produces exemplary results in the quest of restoring sanity unto the lives of patients.

Individual behaviors are based on a series of events that revolve around perceptions. For instance, an alcoholic who wants to reform will feel comfortable in the company of other reformed alcoholics. This sparks the restoration urge that is backed up with emotional responses coming from within. People's interpretation determines how they react to different situations. Agility towards being a sober-minded individual begins with simple steps that support from close family members and friends. CBT relies on individual beliefs, assumptions, and inner thoughts. The overall perception that most patients have determines whether or not the CBT techniques will be successful. Basically, CBT revolves around what people think of themselves as well as on the surrounding environment. A successful Cognitive Behavioral Therapy model should scrutinize the individual perceptions of the patient to determine what triggers certain behaviors and ways of thought. Our feelings have a significant impact on the overall recovery process.

How Social Media Sparks Anxiety and Depression

Social media platforms form is the largest contributor to anxiety and depression in the modern world. Most users compare themselves with those that they meet in these platforms. What they don't know is that a majority of the online users are living a fake life which implicates that they live a good life which may not be true. At the end of the day, the users feel the pressure of wanting to live those fake lifestyles. Research shows that spending most of your time on social media can result in depression that affects your quality of life. The best way of doing this is by making time to form real-time relationships and avoiding fake social media lifestyle. Therapists advise that patients should keep off social media for a speedy recovery. It also keeps them from relapsing into their old habits.

Elements of CBT

CBT works by teaching patients on how they can understand their way of thinking with the aim of restoring their behaviors and thoughts to normality. It teaches the affected parties to be their own therapist for positive results. At the end of any successful therapy, the patients should be in a position to identify what triggers certain behaviors and the impact of such patterns. As a result, the patients become aware of their environment and avoid anything that can make them relapse into their old habits. CBT works on two primary principles: collaborative empiricism and problem-oriented mechanism.

Collaborative Empiricism

This element of CBT requires that the patient and therapist work hand in hand identify the triggers of any abnormal behavior. The main aim of this mechanism is to come up with workable ways on how the patient can avoid those triggers. Besides, it gives the therapist a clear picture of what needs to be done for a successful patient recovery process. A good therapy session focuses on fermenting a functional relationship between the patient and the therapist. This enables the therapist to understand the crucial aspects of the whole treatment program of their patient.

For a speedy recovery process, the patient should open up so that their therapist comes up with an effective plan on how they can restore the patient's health. Trust is vital in any therapy session. You should thus let your therapist know what's bothering you as well as on what triggers certain abnormal behaviors. This gives them a clue about what needs to be done to achieve mental stability. Besides, it creates a beautiful relationship for the team effort to work. Always state your problems with utmost sincerity. Don't hide anything from your therapist because that way, they may come up with a plan that doesn't befit your condition.

Collaborative empiricism thrives on teamwork between the patient and the therapist. In most instances, the therapist will ask a few questions to know the condition of their patients. In some cases, a few tests may be conducted to determine the level of a patient's addiction to harmful substances. Coming out of any habit is a gradual process that should proceed with the utmost care. The patient should, therefore, be willing to share out their problems with the therapist in a bid to make them aware of the finer details of their situation. It enables the therapist to avoid making assumptions while drafting a workable treatment plan for the patient.

Problem-Oriented Mechanism

This CBT element focuses on dealing with the problem at hand. It aims at coming up with workable solutions to any queer behavior that leads to mental depression and any other disorder. As a result, the therapist comes up with a way of ensuring that the patient gradually stops what affects his emotions, thoughts, and behaviors. This process is solely reliant on the attitude of the patient to become stress-free. It requires dedication from the patient's side towards the whole restoration process.

As a patient, you should first accept that you need help. It gives you clear thoughts on what could be the problem as you work towards eradicating any abnormalities. Also, it makes you fathom on the consequences of your behaviors as well as how it affects your close friends and family members. This should be enough motivation as you try to be free of any addiction that may be messing how you carry out specific duties. After accepting your condition, open up to the therapist and let him/her know what you are going through in your quest towards becoming a better citizen.

Problem-oriented mechanism focuses on the current situation of the patient. The therapist should help you come up with realistic goals which should be specific, timely, measurable, and achievable. For instance, if you are suffering from an obsessive-compulsive disorder, the therapist should draft a workable plan on how you reduce the time spent in focusing on one item. This model of CBT concentrates on the problems that are current as well as on how they can be solved in a gradual process. Its aim is to make sure that by the end of a therapy session, the patient is control of certain obsessive behaviors that affect they perceive specific problems. This process is only workable if the patient shows interest in the whole process. It requires that there should be a willingness from both parties with the focus of achieving realistic results within a stipulated amount of time.

Cognitive Behavioral Therapy has been proved successful in treating a variety of psychological disorders such as depression, alcohol, and drug abuse, mental illness, marital issues, and eating and anxiety disorders. When applied effectively, CBT leads to an improvement in the quality of life, which transitions to better performance in other fields. Research shows that CBT provides successful results as compared to other psychiatric therapy tactics. CBT often thrives on changing the thinking patterns of an individual with the aim of completely doing away with any queer behaviors that affect the quality of life of any person. It uses an instigative approach to ensure that patients can think straight and make sober decisions effectively lead to a better lifestyle. CBT focuses on ways of doing away with faulty thinking patterns and coming up with helpful behaviors that prevent patients from going back to their old habits that affect their way of life.

One strategy that CBT uses is to recognize the distortions that cause an individual to indulge in unwanted behavior. Most triggers are avoidable, but the effort towards realizing sobriety in your way of thinking solely relies on the attitude towards being free of any disorders. Therefore, you should clearly understand what spark chains of reactions that ultimately lead to a change of behavior. In most cases, it's the environment that determines how you think and relate with other people. If you are surrounded by negative individuals, your focus will shift from being a better person because of that negativity.

In such instances, you should understand that your behaviors have consequences. You should always think of ways of improving better relationships with your friends and close family members. You may not know it, but some people may be looking up to you as a role model. Thus, any slight deviation from the main course might hurt their feelings. Some may follow your path and end up destroying their future. Before doing anything, always determine its impact on the general environment. What are the benefits of your actions? Do your thoughts endanger the general well-being of every individual? If not, what are you doing to correct that situation?

Let's face it; sometimes, you come across difficult life situations that affect how you think or carry out your daily activities. If you don't speak out, the problems may escalate hence making it difficult to solve the situation at hand. That is why it is imperative to have problem-solving skills that will help you out in such circumstances. These skills become perfect after years of practice, and so, you should often train to line them out. Do the research and determine what affects you the most. After that, draft workable plans on how you'll tackle those problems without compromising on your dignity.

To tackle your problems, you need to be confident and face them without any fear. Always think about the beauty of having clear thought after going through a successful therapy treatment program. Learning to develop your confidence helps, in ensuring that you handle your fears without postponing them for a later date. Postponing problems only makes the situation worse as it goes up beyond manageable levels. This will, in turn, affect your ability to come up with workable solutions to any problem that you are facing. In situations, be calm and partner with a therapist for a successful expedition.

CBT combines both cognitive and behavioral techniques to determine how you think when trying to solve particular problems. Here's how these techniques are applied to come up with workable solutions.

How Cognitive Techniques Work

Before applying cognitive techniques, the therapist makes an attempt to determine how the patient views things. This enables the therapist to understand any alternative assumptions and thus come up with workable solutions to solve such problems. Cognitive techniques are based on Socrative questioning mode between two different parties: the patient and a therapist. This mode of questioning enables the therapist to direct their patient into a specific way of thought while that is deemed fair and workable. It works by first drawing the attention of the patient and then slowly guiding them into practical problem-solving tactics. The therapists use these Socratic questions to determine the patient's assumptions as well as their beliefs and perspectives. This technique gives them an extensive explanation of the behaviors of their patients. The consistent data on observations provides a clear outline of the maladaptive beliefs of the patients as well as how those beliefs impact their way of thought.

The available evidence is enough for a therapist to come up with workable treatment programs. When the patient seems to disagree with the results of the therapist, he/she should back up the claims with any evidence. Dysfunctional assumptions can cause a considerable backlash when attempting to solve physiological problems. The treatment programs should be based on realistic evidence so that they become effective. Therapists should always conduct extensive research to dispel any doubts from the patient's side. A successful treatment plan should focus on patient restoration within the shortest time possible without compromising on the overall results.

How Behavioral Techniques Work

Behavioral techniques focus on activity schedule so that the patient does beneficial and pleasurable activities. The mind works in an exciting way. If you don't replace the event with interesting acting, the patient is more likely to fall back into his/her old ways. Therefore, behavioral techniques work by replacing bad habits with constructive ones. This move enables the patient to focus on new activities that don't jeopardize the efforts of rehabilitation. As such, these techniques create a baseline off what the patient should do daily or weekly to avoid relapsing into his/her old ways.

The behavioral techniques enable the patient to establish new routines that improve the quality of their lives. The techniques are more effective in managing the condition of patients who are suffering from anxiety disorders. It enables the patients to try out new routines to manage their condition. After some time, the patient will find it easy to make time for such activities and thus avoid any life-damaging behaviors. It also enlightens the therapist on the tolerance levels of his/her patient. Some behaviors may be hard to do away with, and thus, the best way is to determine how long the patient can withhold the urge of wanting to use a certain product or perform a harmful task.

Moreover, behavioral techniques help to determine the worst-case scenario on the patient should they stop their harmful lifestyle behaviors. Thus, the therapist will determine all the threats that surround a specific treatment program aimed at health restoration. Behavioral experiments give realistic impressions on the effect of trying to withdraw from unhealthy behaviors. It enables the therapist to keenly supervise their patient and establish any deviations during the treatment program. Most behavioral therapy techniques focus on ensuring that patients relax when performing new routines to replace their old habits with healthy ones.

CHAPTER 2: IMPACT OF COGNITIVE BEHAVIORAL THERAPY

Psychotherapy has transitioned over the years from simple methods to more sophisticated ones. However, studies have shown that most therapists often ignore the effects that CBT may have on the lives of patients. It's is important that all therapists make their patients aware of any impending risks that come with CBT. This prepares the patients physically and emotionally while adjusting to the new conditions that come with the treatment process. The impact of CBT cannot be underestimated, especially because it affects the lives of patients directly.

There is no doubt that cognitive-behavioral therapy has brought a revolution in treating mental illness. The results of CBT are exemplary, especially for the patients who have been suffering from depression, which ultimately lead to mental health problems. But with an effective plan, patients ought to go through the treatment program knowing any possible impacts: negative or positive, that may come along with the whole process. Patients also need to do research on the possible side effects that they might face while undergoing treatment. This enables them to be bold enough and face any problems that they'll face during the restoration plan.

During the treatment program, it's essential that the therapist watch out for any problems that may make the patient relapse to his/her old habits. Once a patient is admitted to your facility, it's extremely important that you guide them through the whole treatment program. Therapists need to be frank with their patients. List down any side effects of the treatment program and go through them with your patient. Answer all the questions that may come up during the discussion and dispel any misconception that the patient might have heard from his/her peers. There is a lot of information that you should clarify on before embarking on the treatment plan. One mistake that is common among most therapists is that they assume that their patients must have conducted research before seeking the treatment services. While some patients are conscious enough to do a little research before embarking on the treatment plan, some need to be enlightened about the whole treatment process. We all want a workable plan for everyone, and every little detail should be made clear for a successful treatment expedition. It saves the time that is normally wasted when patients relapse back to their old habits because they were not prepared enough to tackle their monster.

Advantages of Cognitive Behavioral Therapy

CBT can be used as a successful treatment program to correct mental disorders. Some mental health disorders are so complex that even medicine is not enough to treat them. Many researchers have proved that if used efficiently, CBT can restore the mental health of patients within a short amount of time. There are certain behaviors that come along with our way of life. As such, they end up affecting how we perceive a lot of information. Misinterpreting information can lead one into depression and other mental disorders that they can avoid by attending CBT sessions when such problems arise. However, for the therapy to work, the patients need to show some commitment. It is common to see CBT work for others while it shows resilience in other instances. All these boils down on how patients react to the problems that they face. For CBT to be a success, the patients should show the willpower to continue pushing on even when the journey seems difficult. The end results of this treatment journey are worth waiting for. Any patient should always focus on the beauty of being free and sober again when making fruitful decisions.

Another added advantage is that CBT takes a short duration to show results. Other talking therapies require that the patients undergo through complex procedures before they can see any tangible results. On the other hand, CBT has a well-defined path that guides patients in their recovery quest. Besides, CBT is made in such a way that therapists are always in physical contact with their patients. This enables them to determine the progress of the whole treatment program and make any necessary adjustments if there is need. This makes it one of the best therapy programs that give patients value for their time and money. A successful recovery process requires that patients be supervised on a regular basis to establish a powerful connection while monitoring the treatment process. CBT is structured in a way that the involved parties can always consult to know if they are on the right track. The fact that it checks on the environment of patients to determine the triggers of any disorderly behavior makes it efficient in correcting the mental disorder. It is a time-efficient tool that doesn't come with complex treatment procedures. Within a short period, the patients would start seeing tangible results in their treatment quest.

Besides, CBT can be adjusted to fit different treatment plans. The flexibility makes it efficient in treating different disorderly behaviors. A good treatment plan should understand that every patient comes with different needs. It is, therefore, unwise to assume that all patients require the same treatment. With CBT, a therapist can modify the treatment program to fit the needs of a specific patient. This, in turn, creates a speedy recovery process as well as quick adjustments to the schedules of the affected parties. CBT is versatile in nature and keeps the patients busy as they seek to establish an environment free of any depression and other mental disorders. By the end of any cognitive behavioral therapy session, the patient is often equipped with the necessary tools that they can use to establish a quality way of life. This lifetime tool enables the patients to go through different adversities should they arise in the future. As such CBT is one of the few treatment therapies that equip the patients with the tools that they need in future cases of depression and stress. This is especially important when someone is done with the treatment plan or if they are far away from their therapists.

Disadvantages of Cognitive Behavioral Therapy

The success of CBT relies on the commitment of the patient. A therapist will do all he/she can to keep you on the right track, but it is actually up to you to achieve fruitful results. Those who are not committed to achieving a quality lifestyle are more likely to relapse back to their old habits. It is advisable that you should avoid anything that might trigger your thoughts and drive you back into the old ways that you wanted to avoid. However, should you go back to unhealthy behaviors, you can always bounce back if you show commitment. CBT equips you with lifetime problem-solving skills. Use them to stay afloat and free from anything that keeps on pulling you back to your past. Talk to close family members about your situation and ask them for a helping hand when you are depressed. Talking out relaxes your and build the confidence needed for a successful behavioral correction. Don't be afraid to express your worries and fears because they make you stronger in your sobriety conquest. We all make mistakes at some point, but for CBT to be successful; you should completely avoid anything that compromises your well-being.

Another disadvantage is that CBT only focuses on the current situation and doesn't go in full detail as to what may have caused the problem at hand. Therefore, this makes it easier for the patient to relapse into old behaviors. For instance, one may be depressed because of the kind of treatment that they got in their childhood. The best way of correcting this would be to go back and discover the triggers that caused the current situation. However, most therapists put more emphasis on the current situation instead of tracking the possible causes of the medical condition. Most mental disorders can be traced back to an abusive childhood, bullying, and bias amongst siblings. An efficient treatment system should focus on establishing a permanent solution as well as addressing any past issues that may have led to the problem witnessed on the patient. This is a shortcoming that makes CBT less efficient in solving a variety of mental disorders. For example, if a patient undergoes an abusive childhood, they usually look for avenues of releasing out their pressure. This may then lead to a series of chain reactions that could have been avoided if the therapist checks on the background.

Also, in the initial stages of CBT, the patient may witness withdrawal symptoms that may even cause them to get more depressed. In many cases, the therapists often don't prepare the patients on how to tackle any withdrawal symptoms. If the pressure is too intense, the patients may end up going back to their old behaviors. The best solution is to prepare the patients emotionally. Let them know what they need to do to overcome any relapse temptations. Being prepared enables them to conquer their fears with ease during the treatment process.

CHAPTER 3: UNDERSTANDING COGNITIVE BEHAVIORAL THERAPY

CBT bases its ideology on the fact that there is a connection between an individual's physical sensations, feelings, actions, and thoughts. Negative feelings and thoughts can always trap one in a mental disorder spiteful cycle. Therapists decide on the best practical ways to help in improving a patient's mental health every day.

Therapists on cognitive behavioral therapy focus on understanding current beliefs and thoughts to decide on how they affect an individual's behavior. The thoughts and beliefs of an individual are very critical; therefore, CBT focuses on identifying, and challenging and changing the way people view situations. This is because thoughts always shape how people behave in real life. It works in the following ways;

Talking Away

As a form of talking therapy, CBT focuses on helping an individual change how they perceive or view things in their lives. This way, people are able to develop good behaviors and have positive moods. The therapist and the ailing person closely work together to decide on what they want to achieve at the end of the program. A client is required to actively participate in the program so that their negative perceptions can be easily taken away, thus positively viewing their lives.

Changing Distortions and Perceptions

Cognitive behavioral therapy aims at helping people come up with better ways of how they view things in life. It helps to eliminate negative mindsets that always prevent positive behavioral outcomes. For instance, once a person is depressed, the way they perceive and interpret situations is distorted, thus having some form of negative behaviors towards everything in life. Once an individual's views are distorted, they developed a negative mindset, easily jump into negative conclusions and always viewing situations as problematic. People automatically view situations as negative once they develop fearful thoughts.

Also, cognitive behavioral therapy comes in to challenge these negative thoughts that an individual develops and help them see the real side of things. Therapist's help people reduce their distress by helping them change how they think about the things they come across in life. Clients are helped to see the positive side of things, thus benefiting their own lives and those of people living around them.

The new information that individuals learn in their therapy programs helps them to solve problems they experience in daily life constructively. This is because they eliminate stress and easily control their moods to avoid any negative outcomes.

An instance in which CBT works to eliminate distortions and negative perceptions is when one had visited a dentist in their childhood ages and had some negative experiences, thus developing some dental phobia. This kind of person may live to think that, any time they will visit a dentist they may experience the same pain during the dental procedure. A cognitive-behavioral therapist comes in to help the individual change their perception that since one dental visit was painful, all other procedures will be painful. The therapist and client will work together and eliminate the faulty perception and come up with a strategy where the client will be able to overcome the fear of visiting a dentist.

The following are some of the things an individual learns during a Cognitive Behavioral Therapy program.

Identifying Problems More Clearly

An individual is helped to come up with strategies through which they can go through a problem and solve it adequately other than jumping into conclusions. An individual learns to come up with the best solutions to solve a problem using a positive mindset. They are able to avoid generalizing things but understanding a problem clearly so that they can know what causes it and the best solutions to eliminate it.

Seeing Situations from Different Perspectives

A patient on Cognitive Behavioral Therapy is able to develop positive ways of viewing and thinking about situations. A client is able to view not only the negative sides of a situation but also the positivity in the situation. This way, individuals are able to approach every situation positively and with a positive mindset.

Becoming More Aware of Their Own Moods

A patient who undergoes the CBT program is always able to understand automatic thoughts and how they can positively or negatively change their mood. They are able to get rid of negative thoughts that may lead to bad moods, which may also negatively affect their cognitive behavior. Individuals purpose to focus on the positive side of things so as to lead better lives.

Distinguishing Facts and Irrational Thoughts

The thoughts an individual has always affect their cognitive behavior. In Cognitive Behavioral Therapy, a client learns that there is a clear difference between factual things and what is in their mind. This way, they are able to embrace facts and eliminate the negative mindset they may have in a particular situation. A therapist ensures that a patient understands set principles of dealing with situations and that they are able to apply every time throughout their life.

CHAPTER 4: COGNITIVE BEHAVIORAL THERAPY TECHNIQUES

The Nature of Cognitive Behavioral Therapy

There is a great difference between other psychotherapy sessions and cognitive behavioral therapy. This is because all the sessions involved in the program usually have a set structure. The client and the therapist use a set procedure to tackle the problem they are experiencing. In the initial step, the client and the therapist work together to identify the particular problem and set down the objectives they aim to achieve at the end of the program.

The outlined problems and goals set determine how the sessions will be planned and the content to be discussed in every session. In each set session, they both point out the main topics of discussion and also set aside some time to go through the previous session's discussion.

Homework is given to the client after every session, which is a convenient way of keeping track of the client's progress. The homework plays a significant role in helping the therapist understand the client and how they are viewing things. A therapist may require the client to keep a diary where they record situations that provoke them, causing anxiety and distress. This way, the therapist will be able to understand a client's thoughts and meanings they give to specific situations. The assignments given continue to vary as the therapy session continues. For instance, homework may involve keeping a record of how a client reacts to a situation and the coping mechanism they use to approach it.

Importance of the Set Structure

The CBT program is often short, and the time taken varies according to the condition. Therefore, a structure is important so as to utilize the time set for the program effectively. A structure helps in making sure that each information is tackled without skipping any vital details. It also helps the therapist to keenly track down on the progress of the client as they are able to discuss previous sessions conclusions as well as going through the assignments given to the client. A structure helps the client to easily understand all the basic principles of coping with life situations, thus being able to work on their own.

The relationship that therapists establish with their clients also distinguishes Cognitive Behavioral Therapy from other forms of therapy. The therapist ensures they come up with an equal relationship where, together with the client, they can actively participate in the program. Therapists do not make the clients so dependent by taking up all power of making decisions and giving views on every detail but equally collaborate with the client.

Therapists always apply the "Collaborative empiricism" by Beck while working with their clients. In this case, a client is allowed to give feedback on how they view the therapy programs and the decisions they are about to make. A therapist in this way is able to come up with the best strategies that will fit a client's condition, and that will work best for them.

Cognitive Behavioral Therapy is based on aspects of stoic and philosophy. CBT helps people understand the benefits of feeling calm when faced by catastrophic situations other than teaching them how they should feel. It teaches people about avoiding piling up problems when they experience a negative situation and become upset about it. This is because when an individual approach a situation calmly, one is able to use their knowledge and resources to solve the problem effectively.

Cognitive Behavioral Therapy is based on an Educational Model. The assumptions under which CBT is based that we learn most of our behavioral and emotional reactions are scientifically proven. The therapy, therefore, focuses on helping people overcome their unhelpful thoughts and feelings and teach them new ways of coping with situations. It has some educational advantage in that it has some long-lasting impacts where people are able to understand why and how they are doing well so that they can live positive lives.

CBT theory and techniques used rely on the inductive method. Therapists help their client to base their thinking on facts. This way, they are able to avoid making conclusions on a situation based on what they are thinking, or they may have experienced in the past. Clients are taught on thoroughly analyzing a situation before jumping into conclusions, which is an effective way to maintain positive behavior, attitude, and mood.

Cognitive Behavioral Therapists always give some homework to their clients and encourage them to read and understand as they practice the newly learned approaches every day. They are encouraged not only to think of the techniques learned but also to practice them so that to complete the set program effectively. This way, they are able to achieve the goals they set at the beginning of the therapy program.

Cognitive Behavioral Therapists will always focus on understanding what a client's feels and how they understand particular situations. That is why they use the Socratic Method. In this, clients are allowed to ask themselves questions such as; "how do I know that the teacher is really angry at me?" ": could the teacher be angry at someone else?" Therapists also ask the clients several questions to understand why they perceive things in a particular way.

Steps Involved in Cognitive Behavioral Therapy

A therapist will follow some laid out steps to help in dealing with a client's conditions. The following are the steps taken in a typical session.

Identifying the Troubling Situations or Conditions

The initial step a client will address the issue they are experiencing be it an eating disorder, divorce grief, social phobia, or anger. Together with the therapist, they will be able to decide on what to lay emphasis on during the program.

Awareness of Thoughts, Beliefs, and Emotions about the Problems

The therapist encourages the patient to address their thoughts on a specific problem. The client is required to explain their thoughts about a situation as well as explain how they interpret every experience. A cognitive behavioral therapist may, at some point ask you to put down your thoughts on a book.

Identifying Unhelpful and Negative Thinking

Closely monitoring the patient's reactions to different occurrences helps a therapist to understand one's behavior and thinking. This way, they are able to understand what may be causing the problem the patient is experiencing. The therapist explains this to the patient and makes them understand why they behave in a certain way when faced by a particular situation.

Reshaping Negative Thinking

At this point, the therapist actively engages the patient by asking them several questions to determine whether their reactions are based on facts or on simple assumptions. The therapist helps the client to change their pattern of thinking by teaching them how to tackle and approach different situations. This is because since one situation resulted in being negative does not mean that all other occurrences will be negative. The inaccurate thinking is eliminated, and the fear overcame.

Techniques Used in Cognitive Behavioral Therapy

Cognitive Behavioral Therapy uses practical approaches to solve problems that a patient is experiencing. These approaches help to positively change the cognitive processes of an individual, thus changing their behaviors and improving their mental and physical health. Therapists use proven techniques to help individuals change their feelings, thinking, and behaviors so as to fit in the society. The interventions used are frequently upgraded to enhance their effectiveness in eliminating both psychological and mental disorders.

The following techniques are considered to be the best in improving the mood and behavior of a client.

Cognitive Restructuring Technique

Cognitive restructuring technique involves assisting people in outlining the thinking patterns that make them behave in a certain negative way or experience some unhelpful moods. It helps one to understand the reason behind some negative feelings or moods and giving a thought on some incorrect beliefs behind the reactions. This way, an individual is able to think of the negative thoughts that they experience every moment.

Having a bad mood affects the quality of performance of an individual, thus undermining how they relate with other people at work or in society. Through cognitive restructuring, the bad moods that result in some negative behavior are eliminated or changed. One is taught on the best ways of dealing with situations having a positive mindset.

Albert Ellis came up with the technique of Constructive Restructuring in Cognitive Behavioral Therapy in the 1950s. Since then, the techniques have become a significant part of CBT in changing and controlling negative thoughts. This is because when one has a negative mindset; it is likely that they will have an unpleasant behavior, which is not fit in society.

Applications

Cognitive restructuring technique has proven to be successful in treating many ailments. Some of these include social phobia, depression, Post Traumatic Stress Disorder, relationship issues, and anxiety. It has also proven to be useful to people who have some form of fear when about to speak to a large congregation, allowing one to positively change their mood when experiencing a bad day and positive thinking before going into a job interview. Cognitive restructuring is also useful to help one forego fear of success or failure or even engaging in a difficult conversation.

Steps in Constructive Restructuring

Following the necessary steps helps a client to have the best outcomes from a cognitive behavioral therapy program.

Step 1. Calming Down

Many times, clients stress over the thoughts they want to reconnoiter, making it quite difficult to pay attention to using the technique. It is therefore important to calm themselves down by meditating or breathing deeply. This way, a client is able to calm down, especially when they are frustrated or upset.

Step 2. Identifying the Situation

In this step, the client should clearly give a description of the occurrence that led to a particular mood. This gives the therapist a clue about the surroundings that negatively impact the client.

Step3. Analyzing one's Mood

A client describes the mood that they felt when the situation occurred by writing it down. The mood maybe humiliation, anger, insecurity, or frustration. The mood is the central feelings that the client had during the situation.

Step 4. Identifying Automatic Thoughts

This involves writing down the natural thoughts one had when the mood occurred.

Step 5. Finding Objective Supportive Evidence

In this case, a client should try to think of some facts to base the automatic thoughts on. It helps one to understand what happened and what led to the thoughts clearly.

Step 6. Coming up with objectives that contradict the Evidence

The objectives made in this case should be much fairer than the automatic thoughts made initially.

Step 7. Identifying Fair and Balanced Thoughts

At this point, an individual has already weighed the two views of things. They are able to make a fair decision and get a better view of the occurrence.

Step 8. Monitoring the Present Mood

Following all of the above steps helps in positively changing an individual's mood. One should be able to use the same procedure to solve such similar occurrences in the future. Making positive affirmations is important for one to avoid such experiences.

Exposure Assignment Techniques

Cognitive Behavioral Therapists use this technique by exposing a client to something they have a fear of. This is because by continually avoiding situations that an individual fear, their feelings, and thoughts towards it may never be changed. People will always try to avoid anything that may remind them of a particular negative memory, and the relief provided is temporary, but the fear remains. The technique was developed by Ivan Pavlov, and John Watson in the 1900's basing it on the classical conditioning principles.

Graded exposure therapy works in a way that it reduces the traumatic feelings an individual carry about an object or a situation by systematical exposure to the object or situation. For instance, when an exposure therapist is working with a person who has a fear of snails may ask the client to figure out a snail in their mind. The therapist may continue to ask the client to figure out more intense experiences with the snail as they teach them skills on coping with the scenes and providing great support. When the client reduces the fear of imagining about the snail, the therapist may present the snail in a jar in the room and continue to place it on the hand of the client. This way, the fear of the snail is completely overcoming.

Techniques Used in Exposure Assignment Therapy

There are a number of techniques that are used to help an individual overcome negative responses they give to situations or objects. An exposure therapist always analyzes an individual's problem and come up with the best technique to suit their needs. The following are some of the exposure techniques.

Imaginal Exposure: This technique involves the mental confrontation of a particularly troubling situation or object by figuring it out in their mind. For example, a person who has a great fear of presenting an assignment in front of a class, a therapist may request them to imagine presenting some psychology assignment standing in a class of over a hundred students

Virtual Reality Exposure: In this exposure technique, a therapist combines real-life exposure to a particular fear and imaginative exposure. Therefore, an individual is exposed to a situation that appears factual but is just devised. For instance, a person with height phobia may be required by a virtual reality exposure therapist to take part in going down an emergency exit.

In Vivo Exposure: In this form of graded exposure therapy, a client is exposed to a real situation or object. For example, when dealing with a person with a fear of reptiles is taken by the therapist to a snake park and watches all the reptiles being fed.

Systematic Desensitization: In this technique, an individual is trained in relaxing, developing a hierarchy on anxiety, and being exposed to various items and situations that are feared. The techniques that an individual is taught on relaxing are used to eliminate stress and anxiety when faced with a situation or an object.

Flooding Exposure: The technique is applied in a way that a person is exposed to a particular feared situation or object until the fear is completely eliminated. The exposure is done for a long time as the client learns techniques to cope with the situation.

Prolonged Exposure: This exposure technique is applied in Cognitive Behavioral Therapy to help individuals eliminate the fear of traumatic experiences. Some cognitive processing and psychoeducation are included to help in the process.

Medication: There are some medications that are scientifically proven to reduce some conditions, such as anxiety. These include some benzodiazepines and antidepressants have been successfully used to solve some conditions, thus being recommended by many therapy practitioners.

Conditions That Are Treated Using Exposure Therapy

Exposure therapy has proved to be helpful in the treatment of several psychological conditions. The technique is limited to the following conditions;

- Phobias

- Posttraumatic stress

- Obsessive-compulsive anxiety issues

- Panic attacks

- Acute stress

- Social anxiety

Activity Scheduling Technique

Cognitive Behavioral Therapists use this technique to help individuals who avoid taking part in a number of activities due to being depressed or those who find it quite difficult to complete a duty as they are procrastinating. This way, the energy levels of an individual are reduced, they have no motivation to perform specific tasks, and they tend to live by themselves to avoid bothering other people. Such people may find it better to lie in bed all day other than engaging in any activity.

The technique is designed in a way that clients are encouraged to continuously take part in rewarding activities by coming up with a number of helpful behaviors they engage in. The activity scheduling technique proves to be one of the easiest in cognitive behavioral therapy. Activity Scheduling works by adding more activities that a client can take part in. The main goal of the technique is to improve how one connects with the environment by positively reinforcing activities. Clients are exposed to pleasant activities to improve their mood. When patients engage in these activities, symptoms of depression and anxiety tend to be greatly reduced giving positive outcomes.

Steps in Activity Scheduling

Step 1. Diagnosing Depression

Appropriate tools are used in screening for depression to enhance accuracy in diagnosis. The tools are both in the form of a questionnaire that is self-administered or a depression scale form. The tools can easily be downloaded from the internet and filled to the convenience of a patient.

Step 2. Discussing Activities

After making the diagnosis and confirming that a patient needs some cognitive behavioral therapy, a therapist initiates a discussion on activities that the patient engages in every day, those that they may find pleasure in taking part as well as activities they perceive to be enjoyable. A therapist may also inquire from the patient on the activities that they feel are suitable for them to take part in.

Step 3. Giving the Patient Some Homework

Once patients select the activities, they enjoy taking part in; they are given an assignment of completing all the tasks. The therapist may require the patient to follow a strict schedule of setting aside some time for each specific activity or just participate in an activity of their choice at each particular time. It is, however, important for therapists to help their patients come up with a good schedule through which they can engage in all activities at a specific time as they closely monitor them.

Step 4. Motivation and Encouragement

Activity Scheduling aims to help individuals positively change their everyday routines. There is a need for support, both physical and mental so as to get some positive outcomes. A supportive environment proves to be the best in bringing about required change.

Step 5. Reassess

It is important to closely monitor the mental condition of a patient during activity scheduling. There are necessary tools that therapists use to assess the progress of their patients so as to determine whether they are improving. The progress assessment results help to determine whether more therapeutic measures should be applied to the client, or the technique should be changed, modified, or activities should be added.

Successive Approximation Technique

Psychological practitioners have made a number of researches to come up with the best technique to shape animal and human behavior. Successive approximation involves giving rewards as a form of pleasant reinforcement to encourage positive behavior change. It involves several steps that all lead to desired behavior change.

Successive approximation technique can be used in an instance where you want to train your small baby to use sign language to communicate before they are actually able to speak. This way, the baby will be able to communicate when they feel about eating or drinking something before; they can communicate verbally. It is simply shaping behavior. The idea was developed by B.F Skinner when he used it to train his animals and people during his career.

In every step of the successive approximation, a positive change in behavior is recognized, and a reward is made to the patient by the therapist. Therefore, the desire to continue being rewarded encourages the patient to continue improving their behavior, thus leading to the desired outcomes.

An example of an instance that successive approximation can be used in changing human behavior is helping a child overcome unhealthy eating habits that can lead to obesity, getting rid of drug addiction and promoting good performance at school. Appropriate behavioral change may be achieved when in every time there is a significant behavior change it is rewarded, thus motivating the individual to continue till they get to the desired stage.

Mindfulness Practice Technique

This cognitive behavioral technique is based on Buddhism. Its main aim is to help people stay away from negative things and focus their attention on the current occurrences. The technique has been successfully applied by therapists to help people experiencing depression, drug addiction, anxiety, and stress.

The technique works by using a process through which the attention of a client is focused on what is happening at a particular moment. The following are some of the common benefits of using the mindfulness practice technique.

Decreased stress

Mindfulness practice plays a significant role in reducing stress. This is because it gives an individual some of the best approaches to approach stressors in everyday life. It has proven to a better approach to managing stress and improving how an individual regulate their emotions. By decreasing stress, mindfulness practice helps one to come up with positive stress management strategies, thus having a positive mood all through the day. The benefits can be achieved when the client follows the right techniques in eliminating stress. This can be, for instance, by closing their eyes and remaining silent for some time. The technique is very simple and can be applicable to anyone.

Enhanced Ability to Deal with Illness

Besides, Mindfulness practice has proven to be helpful to people who are chronic and terminal ailments. It may not completely heal them, but they are able to manage the conditions easily. It helps to eliminate stress symptoms and how the patients react to ailments and worry when they experience fatigue. Patients are able to avoid focusing on pain and lead lives with a lot of positivity.

Facilitation of Recovery

Also, mindfulness practice helps patients to move on with life from chronic or possible terminal illnesses. It has proven to be helpful in leading positive lives after a traumatic experience with a particular ailment by eliminating stress and anxiety. It has been helpful in improving spirituality and vigor in a number of cancer survivors.

Decreasing symptoms of depression. Cognitive behavioral therapists apply the mindfulness technique to regulate the emotions of their clients. It has, for a long time, proved its effectiveness as a treatment for depression and anxiety. One is required to come out of the negative thoughts, identify their causes, and embrace them instead of trying to fight them. This way, a patient will be able to regulate their emotions, thus positively coping with and managing depression. Mindfulness is also helpful to people with suicidal thoughts as it helps to eliminate them, and a person is able to look at the positive side of life.

Cognitive behavioral therapists have some laid out tips that help their clients to stick to the mindfulness practice.

- Finding the right motivation and intentions. A large number of clients are often faced by a busy day and may forget on the mindfulness practice schedule. However, with the right motivation and intentions, a patient will always look at the positive benefits they are likely to get from the practice, thus setting aside some time for it.

- Finding the right attention and attitude. Every mindfulness practice will vary from a previous one. Therefore, one should understand that there is no negative way of being mindful.

- Coming up with the right spot and posture. Mindfulness practice requires some proper concentration on present happenings. It is therefore important that a client gets a comfortable and familiar place for the activity. Modification may be important when required. The spot chosen should be safe and free from any sort of disturbances from the outside world.

- Scheduling a routine and sticking to it. For effective outcomes from the mindfulness practice, cognitive-behavioral therapists believe it is important to have a strict schedule on the routine practice. A long-term routine should be outlined in a way that it fits the patient's ability to stick by it.

CHAPTER 5: PRINCIPLES OF COGNITIVE BEHAVIORAL THERAPY

The reason behind the development of cognitive behavioral therapy was to help people with depression, which creates some form of negative thoughts and beliefs about their selves. With this kind of negativity, depressed individuals cannot live healthy lives as they always have a negative attitude towards everything.

Cognitive behavioral therapists come in to teach people with mental disorders to become their own therapists. Therapists equip patients with the right tools to overcome behavioral difficulties and psychological distress to prevent them from becoming more intense. Some of the maladaptive feelings are, for instance, the negative emotions one creates in their mind about themselves and the world they are living in, having faulty thoughts on situations they wrongly judge and unhelpful beliefs.

The cognitive behavioral model points out that there is some interrelation between emotions, thoughts, and behaviors. This is because all three can cause some form of distortion to an individual's health in several ways.

The Principles that Guide Cognitive Behavioral Therapy

Cognitive behavioral therapy (CBT) relies heavily on some principles for it to be effective. These principles are in terms of specifics or non-specifics established by both the specialist and the patient to achieve high efficacy. In cognitive behavioral therapy, the patient practices the key elements while the specialist monitors and tracks the progress.

In the specific principles, the order by which they are carried out is systematic. It creates the structure. Cognitive behavioral therapy works on grounds in which these principles are followed to the latter. It is utterly crucial for these principles to be comprehensive to the patient. Below is elaborate insight on the principles of cognitive behavioral therapy based on the extensive research and practice of the same.

A Breakdown of the Principles of Cognitive Behavioral Therapy

There are three main elements that factor in the principles of CBT. These key elements are:

- Structure Principles

- Cognitive Principles

- Behavioral Principles

A thorough comprehension of these principles allows a smooth transition of the patients undergoing CBT from their specific mental disorder into a healthy mindset.

Structure Principles

Structure principles are centered on the development of cognitive models. The formulation used to create the structure is personalized. Cognitive behavioral therapy centers its efficiency on the structure. The components core to the structure is what makes up the specific principle of CBT. A cognitive model is established by this structure. Specialists use the structure as a framework to understand the current mental distress of the individual. A patient on the formulation becomes aware of the mental difficulties perpetrated by his or her experiences.

The experiences could be brought about by constant negative automatic thoughts rather known as NATs or dysfunctional assumptions. A cognitive model curbs the dysfunctions and allows mental stability, and here is how.

Formulating the Cognitive Process of Treatment

Essentials of a CBT cognitive model are developed using formulation. This can be in different formats. Depending on the severity of the individual's mental disorder, the specialist creates a formulation of the cognitive model. The models are mostly exclusive to fit the particular individual's needs. They can be reused by the specialist in repetitive cases, however not entirely in their original formulation. Formulations ensure authenticity the cognitive models thus creating a better chance of efficiency.

Formulations allow an in-depth understanding of why individuals have specific reactions on specific matters. For instance, in the cases of severe depression, various formulations can determine from which angle the individual may tackle the experience into a healthy mindset. They are the frameworks of the cognitive models. For instance, in depression, the longitudinal formulation mirrors the problem from the early stages of childhood. If a child experienced rejection from parents or an authority figure, they developed core beliefs.

Usually negative, the core beliefs lead to demeaning dysfunctional assumptions. A typical example is an individual verbal confession of his or her lack own of worth. In a later mature stage of life, the beliefs can be triggered by a critical loss to become worse. In such a case, negative automatic thoughts are developed, causing the symptoms of depression.

The cross-sectional formulation analyses an individual's thoughts, feelings, behaviors, and physical indications to determine how severe the mental distress levels are.

Setting Concrete Goals

CBT teaches given individuals how to be their own therapists. Setting concrete goals helps the individual have an understanding of what they are working towards from where they are. Concrete goal setting eliminates maladaptive cognitive patterns as well as behavioral patterns.

A concrete structure develops on each achieved goal. It works on the short term, here and now goals that are crucial to the individual. The formation guides the individual on the types of goals they set. A CBT specialist tracks the progress of the individual by analyzing how the goals were met. CBT focuses on establishing solutions of the here and now mental problems. The goals address current situations of distress and mental breakdown.

Working within Stipulated Time

With any set goals, timelines work to our advantage. Cognitive behavioral therapy works within the shortest stipulated time possible per goal. Achieving high levels of efficiency in CBT materializes during these timelines.

CBT addresses the problems from the point of improving a patient's current state of mind. With the assistance of the specialist, the patient sets smart goals which are;

- Achievable

- Realistic

- Specific

- Measurable

- Time limited

How authentic and genuine a patient is with themselves while setting the goals determines how well they keep the stipulated timeline.

Focus on the Here and Now Problems

Cognitive behavioral therapy focuses on the present problems. The sessions do not take individuals in the root of the problem which most of the time, happens to be in the past. Instead, a cognitive model is created for the patients to be able to understand and solve their immediate problems.

Providing solutions for the immediate problem in CBT defines the concept of the entire therapy. The conventional methods involve digging up the past to find solutions. CBT runs on the principles solving the problems at hand, therefore, creating adequate time to prepare for future adaption into mental wellness.

Patients' Will to Get Better

The culmination of specific principles of the cognitive behavioral therapy narrows down to the will of the patient to get better. An individual's collaboration into obtaining mental wellness determines the efficiency and the time frame of CBT.

Sometimes, patients need to understand the benefits of cognitive behavioral therapy in order for them to align with the principles of the therapy. As much as CBT may be self-therapeutic, the responsible CBT specialist must ensure a patient gets in line with these principles in order for them to achieve better results from cognitive behavioral therapy.

The structure of a cognitive model follows the above principles. However, there are two more major factors to consider. CBT targets the thinking and the behavior of an individual. These are the other two main principles of cognitive behavioral therapy. They are explained below.

Principles of CBT Based On Cognition

Principles of CBT based on cognition are nonspecific. They range from a wide variety of emotional reactions from an individual. We cover a few elements that are crucial for an effective CBT. Previous studies from both the cognitive specialists and the individuals undergoing the therapy show these are the topmost principles based on cognition.

Understanding

Patients need to start therapy from the point of understanding. They should be in a position to comprehend the various benefits of CBT, how it works and the process by which they find mental healing. Understanding the process may sound cliché but in real essence, CBT to take effect in the person's life.

When a patient understands why they react to certain situations the way they do, they are in a better position to rectify that by making better future choices. Understanding goes both ways for the patient and the specialist. To be able to create an effective and suitable formulation for the client, a specialist should strive to get an understanding of why a patient is a way they are.

Cognitive behavioral therapy cannot be a success if either of the parties holds a misunderstanding of any sort involving the therapy.

Rapport

Rapport is another key principle of effective cognitive behavioral therapy. The close and harmonious relationship developed from the point of understanding by both parties enables consistency in communication.

Since CBT relies heavily on communication, a rapport creates an avenue for both the individual and the specialist. The specialist becomes more aware of the needs of the individual through a rapport. An effective formulation is developed as a result of the rapport. However, there are some individuals who struggle with creating this connection with their specialist. These individuals eventually take longer lessons compared to those that establish a rapport in the early stages of the therapy.

Genuineness

Honesty is the best policy. Genuineness displays authenticity. An authentic individual gets an authentic formulation that works magic on their mental distress or dysfunction. Genuineness starts from the inside of a person, which is the emotional aspect. Genuineness fosters the following:

- Respect

- Time saving

- True healing

- Ability to see things in positive perspectives

Genuineness creates trust. From a specialist perspective, a patient will gain their trust when the specialist employs being genuine. In most cases, the individuals open up to the idea of the therapy. The formulation developed in an authentic state become highly effective. Although CBT addresses the current problems, a genuine individual may also find solutions for past problems from simply being genuine. Genuineness implies authenticity to self and the people around you.

Empathy

Severe mental distress/ mental dysfunction can cause an individual to suffer the inability of empathy. In such cases, the individual constantly attends to their maladaptive behaviors. In other cases, patients constantly feed their negative automatic thoughts.

Individuals achieve a higher level of consciousness when they have the ability to understand and share other peoples feeling. Empathy may often sound as vulnerability to people with acute mental distress. However, empathy carries a form of maturity by itself.

It represents mental wellness. An example of mental dysfunctions that kills empathy is narcissism. Narcs are unable to feel empathy for people around them and often come off as cold and rigid, a trait that is constantly harmful to those around them.

Cognitive Behavioral Therapy aims to empower individuals to take control of their psycho-social lives. Under CBT, individuals are able to manage their lives by taking control of their problems. Other principles that are essential to Cognitive Behavioral Therapy include a wide range of behavioral techniques.

Principles of CBT Based on Behavioral Techniques

Cognitive behavioral Therapy sets attainable goals on the behavior patterns of an individual. The goals are achieved on a set of therapeutic behavioral principles. Here are a few of the most common cognitive behavioral principles in the therapy.

CBT method of self-treating uses open dialogue to come up with solutions that are best suitable for the specific individual. Collaborative dialogue involves a series of questions that enable the therapists to create a comprehensive formulation. Socratic questioning stimulates the patient's consciousness into focusing on the problem-solving techniques rather than the problems.

Due to its nature and focus on helping individual's lead better lives, a set of principles guides CBT. Following these principles helps cognitive behavioral therapists to empower individuals to have some control over their own lives using the appropriate techniques. The following are the guidelines of cognitive behavioral therapy.

1.   Cognitive Behavioral Therapy is Educative

Cognitive behavioral therapy focuses on teaching a patient to become their own therapist. This means that the therapists help the clients learn their current ways of thinking and behavior and how they are affecting their lives. CBT focuses on teaching the clients how each belief or though can lead to a particular disorder they may be suffering from. It aims to help these people understand that some thoughts they have may not be factual, thus being entirely unhelpful to them and causing more distress.

Patients are given the right tools that help them to overcome maladaptive patterns of behavior. They are helped to understand how to utilize the tools to approach any challenge that may be causing particular distress to them. Sessions in cognitive behavioral therapy are held just as in a classroom whereby both the therapist asks the clients some questions; they answer and hold some form of discussion for better understanding. Homework is also given to the client by the therapist to help in tracking down their progress after each session.

A patient is required to take home therapy notes on every therapy session. The notes help the client to continue practicing behavioral change.

2.   Cognitive Behavioral Therapy is based on the Establishment of a Collaborative Therapeutic Relationship

The form of relationship that is created during the therapy sessions sets CBT aside from other types of therapy. The relationship is collaborative and focuses on being mutual. In this case, the therapist does not assume all the power of asking and answering questions but makes the clients participate in the program actively. The therapist and the patient always work together as a team so that they can check on the maladaptive thoughts and beliefs, check on how valid they are and together put the effort in trying to rectify them.

In this case, a client is given the freedom of expressing how they feel about a situation or an object and how they would like it to be dealt with. The client also feels a sense of confidence due to the collaborative nature of the program. This way, they are able to describe a problem without fear and clearly understand the techniques to tackle the issues.

3. The Focus of Cognitive Behavioral Therapy is Problem-Focused and Goal-Oriented

Cognitive-behavioral therapy focuses on what is happening at the present moment. This means that it looks at the current problems and difficulties, and an individual may be experiencing and not what happened in the past that could be affecting an individual's behavioral patterns. CBT focuses on getting ways on improving the current state of mind of clients to help them in living healthy lives.

To solve the problems, CBT involves a collaborative client and therapist goal setting. Through the goals set, the therapist is able to focus on ways through which the client's problem can be solved appropriately. The therapists assist the patients in prioritizing the goals they want to achieve by breaking down the disorder they are going through and coming up with a hierarchy of smaller goals they would like to accomplish at the end of the session.

4. Sessions in Cognitive Behavioral Therapy are Structured

Structuring the sessions helps in increasing the efficiency of the treatment programs. The initial stage of structuring the sessions involves setting an agenda for the program. In this process, the therapist and the client decide on the items that will help in making the therapeutic work much productive and useful.

Having a set agenda to tackle in every session makes the process of learning and understanding much easier for the client. It also improves how the program is held as each set agenda set has its own set time. Furthermore, homework is given to the client enhancing their efforts in the treatment process. They are able to understand the techniques taught by practically utilizing them outside the therapeutic environment.

5.   Cognitive Behavioral Therapy is Time-Limited

Time limitation is one of the things that make cognitive behavioral therapy different from other forms of treatment. It is not open-ended as in other talk therapies. CBT has the aim of terminating the program at a particular time when the patient is conversant and competent to practice it on their own. The program takes the utmost 16 weeks. The patient is expected to reasonably understand and become conversant with the skills they are being taught in the first eight weeks.

After the eight weeks, the patient usually shows a decrease in the symptoms they showed to cause some distress to their mental health. In the remaining weeks, they practice the techniques taught to ensure the symptoms are entirely eliminated. However, the severity of a disorder spells the amount of time it is going to take for a patient to completely heal. For long-lasting impacts, such people require additional therapy sessions.

Time limitation in cognitive behavioral therapy means that once a patient shows some form of relief and the techniques appropriate for success, the treatment program is ended. This way, the session becomes significantly brief than other traditional forms that can take more than a year.

6. Cognitive Behavioral Therapy is based its ideas on an ever-evolving formulation of the patients and their problems in cognitive terms

This principle is based on three major things about the patient. In the initial stages of the session, the therapist is likely to consider the current thinking of the client that may lead to the negative feelings they are having. For instance, in the case of a client who feels anxious and depressed, the therapist will first look at their current thinking. The client may be thinking that he is a failure and will never be happy in life. This kind of feeling may contribute to some maladaptive behavior in the patient, thus doing nothing productive and spending a whole time lying in bed. This is because of the dysfunctional thoughts reinforced by maladaptive behavior.

The second thing to be considered is the participating factors. These are the factors that may be influencing some maladaptive behavior in an individual. For instance, the contributing factor to the above patient's depression, maybe because of being far away from their loved ones and struggling to succeed in business, making them feel quite incompetent.

Thirdly cognitive-behavioral therapists look at the critical developmental events and enduring patterns that the clients use to interpret the events. This involves looking at some of the things that may have actually led to depression. For the above patient's the cause of the recession may be due to some belief that they base success on individual strength and good luck but views his own failures as a weakness in themselves.

The conceptualization of the information a client gives is based on psychological information on depression and the knowledge that a client provides when they are evaluated. In every structured session, the therapist continues to acquire more information and helps the client view their situation in a cognitive model. The client learns how to change their thoughts and acquire more adaptive solutions to tackle distress and challenges he may face in life. This way, the client can act more productively.

7.   Cognitive Behavioral Therapy Requires Sound Therapeutic Alliance

People with mental disorders are likely to have some form of mistrust to the therapists they are working with. The therapeutic alliance created at the initial stage of a cognitive behavioral therapy session determines its outcome. It is the form of trust that is created between the therapist and the patient allowing them to work together effectively. It helps the patient to understand that their therapists have the best interests at heart and are trustworthy.

Therefore, cognitive behavioral therapists are guided by the principle of sound therapeutic alliance where they aim to demonstrate some necessary skills during counseling. The patient should gain the confidence of talking to the therapist and feel relieved after the session. For instance, they are expected to create a good rapport with the clients by showing empathy, warmth, caring, competence, and genuine regard. Genuine regard is one of the essential elements in therapeutic sessions whereby the therapists make some positive statements to the clients and showing them that the therapist clearly understands what they are going through.

Active and careful listening helps a client to feel that they are talking to a caring person and that the feelings are being understood. A cognitive behavioral therapist also summarizes the thoughts of a client accurately for easier description and understanding.

A patient may, at some point during the session become angry at the therapist, but they should be able to continue working as a team productively. The therapist should apply the necessary skills to calm down the patient and continue with the session as planned. They should do this by giving them a pleasing sense that they understand the mental problem that brought the client to the therapy session.

In cases where clients feel incompetent, a therapist should point out to some of their successes, both small and larger ones. This helps the clients to see some optimism in their life, thus positively changing their outlook of things. Asking for feedback after every session helps the therapist to point out the things the client is yet to understand and discuss them once more. This way, the positivity of outcomes is guaranteed.

Cognitive Behavioral Therapy utilizes a variety of Techniques to Change Thinking, Mood and Behavior

Cognitive-behavioral therapists are guided by specific techniques that assist in challenging the patterns of behavior, beliefs, and thinking of a client. A therapist works closely with the patient to understand some of the feelings and thoughts that may be causing stress and decides on the best technique to apply to solve their condition. Majority of the beliefs that clients have are faulty, thus negatively impacting how they function usually.

Choosing the right technique to treat a patient's problem helps to change how they think to change how they feel, which results in a change in the way they view and approach challenges in life. This way, they are able to handle flawed thoughts that lead to anxiety, social phobia, emotional eating that could lead to obesity and depression.

Following the cognitive behavioral therapy techniques

appropriately gives patients the right tools too calmly and accurately approach situations they are faced with without jumping into conclusions. Clients are able to deal with the situation without making flawed assumptions and judgments. It makes them feel relaxed and live happier lives.

How It Works

Cognitive-behavioral therapy works by pointing out to some faulty thoughts that are consistent in a patient and using them as signs for a positive action needed, then replacing the thoughts with much healthier and productive solutions. Cognitive-behavioral therapy has a primary objective of teaching individuals how to cope and manage situations skillfully and changing the automatic thoughts that come up in their minds when a situation arises. It helps patients to gain skills in rational self-counseling when faced by a frustrating or disappointing event.

During the CBT treatment session, the willingness of the patient to cooperate effectively with the therapist determines how easily they can be treated. The patient should actively participate in the program, be ready to have unbiased thoughts, and always work on the assignments given to them by the therapist. The client is expected to remain patient all through the program to provide the therapist with enough time to guide them through the healing process.

Characteristics that Make Cognitive Behavioral Therapy Effective and Unique

Rational Approach

The theory of cognitive behavioral therapy and techniques depend on rational thinking. This means that they focus on researching and using actual facts when dealing with patients. This way, they give patients some time to explore their thoughts and find out whether they are basing their opinions on facts or just faulty assumptions. Therapists help clients to identify the flawed assumptions that make them to distress over a situation or an object,

Law of Entropy and Impermanence

Cognitive-behavioral therapy bases all its assumptions on scientific information. On the law of entropy, it is a sure thing that when something is not used, it is eventually lost. Therefore CBT places some belief in the fact that anyone has the ability to change how they feel or think about something because the power of change rests in their own brains. Once a person changes what they think of something, the mind will always adjust to fit the thoughts of an individual. CBT focuses on helping people think positively, thus leading happier lives in the future.

They Accept Unpleasant or Painful Emotions

Talking therapies help clients to only positively handle and react to challenging situations. However, cognitive-behavioral therapy teaches clients how to embrace and accept challenging conditions. This is because life will not always be smooth, challenges will always occur, and patients should be prepared to avoid judging situations wrongly, which makes them more difficult. Wrong judgments may make one develop self-blame that may turn out to self-hatred leading to depression. Cognition behavioral therapy focuses on teaching patients to accept the situation as part of the vicious cycle of life.

Questioning and Expressing

Cognitive behavioral therapy focuses on asking patients numerous questions and giving them a chance to express their feelings. This is unlike in other therapies where all power of the session may lie on the hands of the therapist. CBT creates a mutual discussion with the patient enabling them to learn new perspectives efficiently. Patients are able to view situations from a positive side and in a realistic way, thus changing their maladaptive pattern of thoughts.

Specific agendas and techniques. Cognitive behavioral therapy sets out an agenda and techniques to be used in every session. This way, the client gets to learn specific things to apply when faced by a particular situation that depresses or distorts their thoughts. The techniques learned can also be used after the formal therapy sessions are over.

Qualities of a Good Cognitive Behavioral Therapist

Cognitive behavioral therapy is guided by some principles and techniques so that the set goals can be achieved. It is therefore vital for a therapist to carry with them some personal qualities, habits, and attitudes so that they can improve their competency when dealing with the clients. When a therapist portrays good personality, all the principles set for CBT can be utilized appropriately.

The following are some of the characters a good therapist should portray.

Show Some Respect for a Patient's Time

At the start of a therapy session, the therapist and the patient always schedule a time for each particular session. It is important that a therapist conform to the set time and consistently communicate with the client when anything changes. It is also crucial that the therapist makes a point of answering the patient's calls and text messages or e-mails. A good therapist understands that a patient may have some demanding things in life barring them from attending sessions on time; thus, should be able to answer their calls promptly.

Being Professional, Ethical, and Showing Respect for Cross-Cultural Issues and Beliefs

This is a broad perspective as it includes the kind of personality the therapist portrays towards the patient. The therapists should be able to maintain a professional boundary as well as be compassionate, caring, and friendly to the patient. All essential requests that may be uncomfortable should be addressed in a calm manner to avoid frustrating or developing some mistrust in the client. The therapist should also remain sensitive to the cultural beliefs of the patient and respectfully communicate with them.

Cognitive behavioral therapy does not only provide instructions but gives some hope and inspiration to the patient. There are many patients who feel hopeless and helpless in life. Providing instructions only may not be so helpful to such patients. Cognitive behavioral therapists always try to instill some hope and confidence to their patients. They do this by leaning in and speaking to these patients in a way they feel minded. Positive feedback plays a crucial role in giving a patient a sense of self-belief, even when they have self-doubt. The patient should be able to remain committed to achieving more meaningful goals in life, even when faced with adversity. Positive energy should be felt in the therapeutic discussion.

Creativity always brings some enjoyment in the therapy sessions. Using creative arts to describe situations helps to create a positive impression in a patients mind. It an incredible way of assisting the clients in sticking some ideas in mind and remembering them even after the formal therapy session. Some of the best things a cognitive-behavioral therapist can use are metaphors, descriptive stories, analogies, and hypothetical questions that can easily relate to the personal experiences of a patient are incredible learning instruments.

Being open and eager to continue learning. As a therapist, one is likely to come across a vast number of people with a lot of things one can learn from them. A cognitive behavioral therapist is expected to have an open mind on lessons about life. They can accommodate patients from different cultures and backgrounds and deals with them equally. The patients may come to the therapist to learn on coping with life situations, but the therapist can also learn about life itself from the patient.

A patient will always take great pride whenever a therapist thanks them for sharing some wisdom and knowledge on life. The patient's ideas can always benefit the therapist both on personal and professional life. Learning how different people from different cultures act on situations helps the therapist to have some diverse approach when dealing with clients. They are able to understand ideologies that may not be beneficial to a patient, thus using the appropriate one in the treatment process.

CONCLUSION

Basically, some of the things that make cognitive behavioral therapy so popular are the extensive studies that are done on it. Many people consider using it due to its modality and the use of brief and goal-oriented interventions to solve problems. Cognitive behavioral therapy focuses on making measurable positive changes to patient's patterns of thoughts and emotions, thus changing their behavior. A patient is always able to see some quick results, thus proving the efficiency of cognitive behavioral therapy. At the end of a cognitive therapy session, a patient can develop unique strategies to approach any form of fear they experience in everyday life.   It is, therefore, important for people who experience some feelings of distress and anxiety that may lead to undesired behavior to seek cognitive behavioral therapy medication.

www.ingramcontent.com/pod-product-compliance
Lightning Source LLC
Chambersburg PA
CBHW061727250726
48657CB00002B/812